Now yo
clarinet
rec

TAKE
THE
LEAD

clarinet

NUMBER ONE HITS

IMP

International
MUSIC
Publications

International Music Publications Limited
Griffin House 161 Hammersmith Road London W6 8BS England

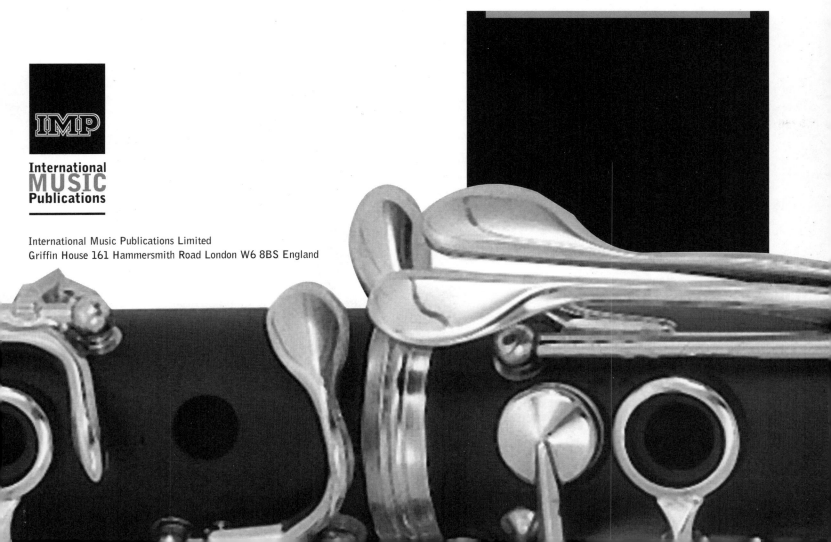

Series Editor: Sadie Cook

Editorial, production and recording: Artemis Music Limited
Design and production: Space DPS Limited

Published 2000

International **MUSIC** Publications

International Music Publications Limited

England:	Griffin House 161 Hammersmith Road London W6 8BS
Germany:	Marstallstr. 8 D-80539 München
Denmark:	Danmusik Vognmagergade 7 DK1120 Copenhagen K

Italy:	Nuova Carisch Srl Via Campania 12 20098 San Giuliano Milanese Milano
Spain:	Nueva Carisch España Magallanes 25 28015 Madrid
France:	Carisch Musicom 25 Rue d'Hauteville 75010 Paris

WARNER BROS. PUBLICATIONS U.S. INC.

USA:	15800 N.W. 48th Avenue Miami, Florida 33014

Australia:	3 Talavera Road North Ryde New South Wales 2113
Scandinavia:	P.O. Box 533 Vendevägen 85 B S-182 15 Danderyd Sweden

clarinet

TAKE THE LEAD

In the Book...

On the CD...

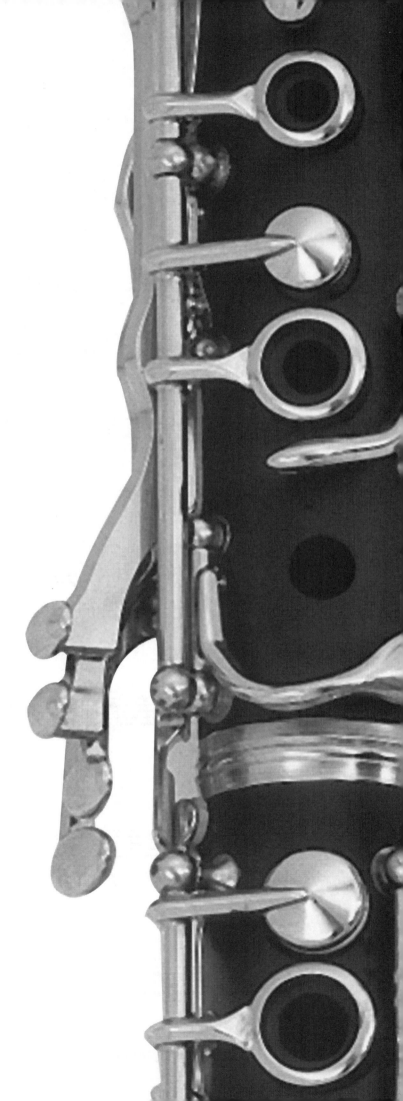

Demonstration

Backing

Believe

Words and Music by
Brian Higgins, Stuart McLennan, Paul Barry,
Stephen Torch, Matt Gray and Tim Powell

When You Say Nothing At All

Words and Music by
Paul Overstreet and Don Schlitz

Demonstration   Backing

Demonstration

Backing

Careless Whisper

Words and Music by
George Michael and Andrew Ridgeley

Demonstration   Backing

Dancing Queen

Words and Music by Benny Andersson,
Stig Anderson and Björn Ulvaeus

Demonstration

Backing

Flying Without Wings

Words and Music by
Steve Mac and Wayne Hector

Demonstration

Backing

I Will Always Love You

Words and Music by
Dolly Parton

Livin' La Vida Loca

Words and Music by
Robi Rosa and Desmond Child

Demonstration

Backing

Demonstration   Backing

You Needed Me

Words and Music by
Randy Goodrum

Printed and bound in Great Britain 7/00

You can be the featured soloist with
TAKE THE LEAD

Collect these titles, each with demonstration and full backing tracks on CD.

90s Hits

The Air That I Breathe (Simply Red)
Angels (Robbie Williams)
How Do I Live (LeAnn Rimes)
I Don't Want To Miss A Thing (Aerosmith)
I'll Be There For You (The Rembrandts)
My Heart Will Go On (Celine Dion)
Something About The Way
You Look Tonight (Elton John)
Frozen (Madonna)

Order ref: 6725A – Flute
Order ref: 6726A – Clarinet
Order ref: 6727A – Alto Saxophone
Order ref: 6728A – Violin

Movie Hits

Because You Loved Me (Up Close And Personal)
Blue Monday (The Wedding Singer)
(Everything I Do)
I Do It For You (Robin Hood: Prince Of Thieves)
I Don't Want To Miss A Thing (Armageddon)
I Will Always Love You (The Bodyguard)
Star Wars (Main Title) (Star Wars)
The Wind Beneath My Wings (Beaches)
You Can Leave Your Hat On (The Full Monty)

Order ref: 6908A – Flute
Order ref: 6909A – Clarinet
Order ref: 6910A – Alto Saxophone
Order ref: 6911A –Tenor Saxophone
Order ref: 6912A – Violin

TV Themes

Coronation Street
I'll Be There For You (theme from Friends)
Match Of The Day
(Meet) The Flintstones
Men Behaving Badly
Peak Practice
The Simpsons
The X-Files

Order ref: 7003A – Flute
Order ref: 7004A – Clarinet
Order ref: 7005A – Alto Saxophone
Order ref: 7006A – Violin

Christmas Songs

The Christmas Song
(Chestnuts Roasting On An Open Fi
Frosty The Snowman
Have Yourself A Merry Little Christma
Little Donkey
Rudolph The Red-Nosed Reindeer
Santa Claus is Comin' To Town
Sleigh Ride
Winter Wonderland

Order ref: 7022A – Flute
Order ref: 7023A – Clarinet
Order ref: 7024A – Alto Saxophone
Order ref: 7025A – Violin
Order ref: 7026A – Piano
Order ref: 7027A – Drums

The Blues Brothers

She Caught The Katy And Left Me A
Mule To Ride
Gimme Some Lovin'
Shake A Tail Feather
Everybody Needs Somebody To Love
The Old Landmark
Think
Minnie The Moocher
Sweet Home Chicago

Order ref: 7079A - Flute
Order ref: 7080A - Clarinet
Order ref: 7081A - Alto Saxophone
Order ref: 7082A - Tenor Saxophone
Order ref: 7083A - Trumpet
Order ref: 7084A - Violin

Latin

Bailamos
Cherry Pink And
Apple Blossom White
Guantanamera
La Bamba
La Isla Bonita
Livin' La Vida Loca
Oye Mi Canto (Hear My Voice)
Soul Limbo

Order ref: 7259A - Flute
Order ref: 7260A - Clarinet
Order ref: 7261A - Alto Saxophone
Order ref: 7364A - Piano
Order ref: 7262A - Trumpet
Order ref: 7263A - Violin

Jazz

Birdland
Desafinado
Don't Get Around Much Anymore
Fascinating Rhythm
Misty
My Funny Valentine
One O'Clock Jump
Summertime

Order ref: 7124A - Flute
Order ref: 7173A - Clarinet
Order ref: 7174A - Alto Saxophone
Order ref: 7175A - Tenor Saxophone
Order ref: 7179A - Drums
Order ref: 7178A - Piano
Order ref: 7176A - Trumpet
Order ref: 7177A - Violin

Swing

Chattanooga Choo Choo
Choo Choo Ch'Boogie
I've Got A Gal In Kalamazoo
In The Mood
It Don't Mean A Thing
(If It Ain't Got That Swing)
Jersey Bounce
Pennsylvania 6-5000
A String Of Pearls

Order ref: 7235A - Flute
Order ref: 7236A - Clarinet
Order ref: 7237A - Alto Saxophone
Order ref: 7238A - Tenor Saxophone
Order ref: 7239A - Trumpet
Order ref: 7240A - Violin